DID ROMANS REALLY
WASH THEMSELVES
IN WEE?

DID ROMANS REALLY WASH THEMSELVES IN WEE?

Dr Dino's Learnatorium

DINO

Published by Dino Books,
an imprint of John Blake Publishing Ltd,
3 Bramber Court, 2 Bramber Road,
London W14 9PB, England

www.johnblakepublishing.co.uk

www.facebook.com/Johnblakepub ⓕ
twitter.com/johnblakepub ⓔ

First published in paperback in 2014

ISBN: 978-1-78219-915-1

British Library Cataloguing-in-Publication Data:

A catalogue record for this book is available from the British Library.

Design by www.envydesign.co.uk

Printed in Great Britain by CPI Group (UK) Ltd

1 3 5 7 9 10 8 6 4 2

Papers used by John Blake Publishing are natural, recyclable products made
from wood grown in sustainable forests. The manufacturing processes conform
to the environmental regulations of the country of origin.

Every attempt has been made to contact the relevant copyright-holders,
but some were unobtainable. We would be grateful if the appropriate
people could contact us.

Introduction

Humans think they know a lot about history. I'm sure in your classes at school you have learned all about the ancient Romans and how they tried to take over the world, or about how the Egyptians built the pyramids, or about the First and Second World Wars and 'important' things like that.

But what you forget is how young you all are – modern humans have only been around for a puny 200,000 years, and have been the dominant species on Earth for much less than that. Us dinosaurs on the other hand were around 230 million years ago. *And* we were dominant for 135 million years. To put into perspective how new humans really are, if you imagine the Earth as being one year old then Homo Sapiens (that's you) have only been around for about 7.5 minutes, and the pyramids were built only 7 seconds ago.

I know humans though. I've lived with them my whole life, and I know you won't be interested in the really massive events that I could tell you about, like the First Tyrannosaurus Wars or the Great Plague of 10,587,649, because they don't involve you. Instead, you want to know about the exploding King of England, grisly human sacrifices, and the real Count Dracula, right? Well I can tell you that, and a lot of other pretty cool stuff you probably won't hear in class. So read on...

Dr Dino

Chaotic Cavemen

Cavemen lived during the Stone Age (so-called because tools were made out of stone), which was between 3.4 million and 5,000 years ago. Even though we think of them as humans, most weren't Homo Sapiens. There were many other species, like the Neanderthals, which were all very similar to each other.

There are more people living in caves now than there have been at any other time in the Earth's history.

The average age a caveman lived to was only 16 years old. So, more of a caveboy really!

Language was still developing throughout the caveman period and a result of this is our yawn. It's believed that yawning was used to show all the members of your caveman group that you were tired and it was time for bed. This is why it is still contagious today – when caveman yawned, all the others would follow suit.

Cavemen wouldn't have just one cave. They were nomads, which meant that they would travel around and find new caves to live in quite often, for example if the weather became too cold, or if they ran out of easy access to food or water.

The oldest human fossils are 400,000 years old and were found in a cave in Northern Spain called 'The Pit of Bones'.

Dr Dino's Dino Movies

It can be very frustrating for dinosaur doctors like me when movies like *The Flintstones* or *Ice Age* show dinosaurs living alongside humans. THIS NEVER HAPPENED! The only dinosaur that ever lived with humans is me, and I'm a pretty special case.

Cavemen often painted the caves that they lived in and, incredibly, some of these paintings still survive today. One of the most famous of these is the Lascaux cave in

France, which has nearly 2,000 images. Most paintings are of animals, and quite a few people think they were just cavemen showing off and making a record of what they had hunted, much like people might take a picture now.

Awful Aztecs

It's easy to think of the Aztecs as pretty ancient, but in fact they only arrived in modern-day Mexico in the 1300s. Before that the Mayans had been in charge for a long time...

The Miserable
Mayans

The Mayans famously created a calendar system that predicted that the world would end on 21 December 2012. For some reason, even though the Mayans were long gone by this time, some people still believed them and 'end-of-the-world' parties happened all around the globe on that date. One person who probably wasn't celebrating was Dutchman Pieter van der Meer who had an ark installed in his back garden in readiness. Still, at least he's got a nice big boat to play in now!

They weren't the cheeriest lot, the Mayans. They built huge pyramids dedicated to their gods, which was nice. But they used the pyramids for human sacrifice, which wasn't... Often, the priests in charge would cut the heart right out of the victim while he was still alive!

Being a Mayan kid wasn't too fun either. If the adults thought your head was too broad they would put two

planks of wood on either side to push on your head and make it narrower.

For some reason in the 900s the Mayans all fled the cities and left them abandoned. Many explanations have been given for this, ranging from a peasant revolt (probably against all the priests cutting out their hearts!), overpopulation leading to famine, a huge earthquake or a devastating plague. The truth is, much like the dinosaur extinction, nobody really knows. (Except me, of course. I could tell you all about what happened to the dinosaurs, but nobody ever asks me.)

Dr Dino's Favourite Fact

Apparently modern humans aren't the only ones who think egg-heads are clever. Archaeologists were puzzled when they found funny-shaped skulls that looked exactly like eggs but they figured out that the Mayan leaders wore headgear to reshape their skulls to make them real egg-heads!

Back to
the Aztecs

The Aztecs learned quite a lot from the Mayans – not least the old trick of human sacrifice. And they were pretty 'bloody' good at it too. It's believed that they sacrificed an average of 50,000 people a year, and in one massive party to celebrate opening the temple in their capital of Tenochtitlan they killed 20,000 people in honour of the sun god.

The Aztecs never actually called themselves the Aztecs. Western historians came up with that description – they called themselves the Mexica.

Even worse than human sacrifice, the Aztecs were very cruel to their kids. They introduced…*Compulsory Schooling!* If you were low-born you had to learn to be a warrior if you were a boy and how to be a housewife if you were a girl. The worst off were the nobles who had to learn maths, art, history and politics.

When two Aztecs got married, they would tie the man and woman's clothing together. This is believed to be the origin of the phrase 'tying the knot'.

Mexican food, like fajitas and quesadillas, can be delicious, but you might have wanted to give some Aztec foods a miss... They would eat everything from monkeys and dogs to toads and frogs. And they were even known to make cake from pond scum!

Hernan Cortes and his Spanish army are often given the credit for conquering the Aztecs in 1519 by military brilliance. (That, plus the fact that they had guns while the Aztecs only had spears!) However, the real killer was something the Spaniards brought with them – smallpox. The disease tore through the Aztec population, which hadn't ever been exposed to it before, and allowed Cortes and his men to take over.

The Greatest Explorers

It wasn't too long ago that people thought the world was flat. (Or even weirder: that it rested on the back of a giant turtle!) But despite this, some brave (or very stupid) men set off to travel the high seas to see if they would fall off the edge. Here are the top 10 greatest explorers of all time:

10. Vasco da Gama – He discovered the route to sail directly from Europe to India (around the bottom of Africa). He looked after himself pretty well, but it wasn't so great to be one of his sailors – more than half of them died of scurvy on the trip, including his brother!

9. Ferdinand Magellan – Magellan's expedition sailed the whole way around the world, doing piddling things like naming the Pacific Ocean along the way. He would be higher up the list but, due to a combination of bad diplomacy and sharp spears, he was killed in the Philippines and never made it home.

8. Robert Fitzroy and Charles Darwin – Fitzroy was the captain of HMS *Beagle*, the ship that took Darwin to the Galapagos Islands where he first came up with the little idea of evolution. The only reason Darwin came was for a bit of conversation – the captain before Fitzroy had got so bored he had killed himself!

7. Stanley and Livingstone – David Livingstone was an explorer and national hero who went deep into the unknown heart of Africa and discovered a lot of it. Unfortunately, he wasn't as good as he thought he was and he got lost! Henry Stanley was sent to find him and finally did (after a couple of years!). When he eventually tracked him down all he said was 'Dr Livingstone, I presume?'

6. Christopher Colombus – He famously discovered America, (although try telling that to the Native Americans!). In fact, Colombus was convinced that he had landed in Asia, however he soon realised his mistake. He never set foot on mainland America himself, but on his first trip there he left 40 people in a settlement. By the time he came back, they were all dead.

5. Lewis and Clark – This pair of hardy explorers spent a couple of years crossing the unknown America, mapping the vast wilderness as they went. The mission was a great success, except for one hairy moment when they sent a man travelling with them, Cruzatte – who only had one eye – out hunting. He mistook Lewis for an elk and shot him right in the bum. Lewis survived, but he had trouble sitting for the rest of the trip.

4. Leif Ericson – Leif is probably the greatest explorer to get the least credit for it. He was a Viking who made it all the way to America, 500 years before Colombus! Unfortunately for him, all evidence suggests he was pretty peaceful and, unlike later Europeans, didn't try to conquer anyone. Consequently, everyone forgot all about him and nobody believed he'd actually made it until 1963, when archaeologists discovered an old Viking village right where he said he'd been.

3. Captain Cook – Not to be confused with the equally famous Captain Hook, James Cook had the pleasure of sailing the Pacific and discovered countries such as Australia and New Zealand. One of the people who paid for his journey was Lord Sandwich, and Cook tried to repay him by naming Hawaii the Sandwich Islands. But

the name didn't stick, and it seems the Hawaiians didn't much like it either – on his third trip there they got in a fight and Cook was killed!

2. Marco Polo – Marco Polo was a 13th-century explorer who travelled around most of Asia. He's often seen as the grandfather of all explorers. The only reason we know so much about it is because he had a bit of time on his hands… When he headed home to Italy there was a war going on and he was on the wrong side. Marco was thrown in prison and was so bored he decided to write his story.

1. Neil Armstrong – The ultimate explorer, it was a 'great leap for mankind' when Armstrong became the first man to walk on the moon in 1969. And he finally proved once and for all that it wasn't made of cheese.

The Glorious Greeks

The Greeks were pretty clever chaps. Unlike their rivals the Romans, they never had big dreams of conquering the world (except for Alexander the Great, but more about him later), however they were great inventors and traders, and they spread knowledge throughout the known world better than anyone else. From around 1600 BC until the Greeks became part of the Roman Empire in 146 BC the Greeks were without a doubt the most glorious of the lot.

The Greeks invented or discovered an incredible number of things. Among them were the first maps as we know them, the discovery of most of the other planets in our solar system, coming to the realisation that there was science behind illnesses, figuring out that the Earth is a globe, inventing central heating and creating the world's first democracy. And, most importantly, creating the first flushing toilet! Unfortunately, they were so far ahead of everybody else that when they weren't around most of their best stuff was forgotten, and it was nearly 2,000 years later that people re-invented a lot of it.

Toasting at parties first began in ancient Greece. The host would always drink first, and his guests would wait until after he'd done so to have their drinks. They weren't being polite... they were making sure that the drink wasn't poisoned!

Dino's Olympics

People are always telling me that the Greeks were the first to create the Olympics. There were all sorts of different competitions, but the most dangerous was definitely the Pankration – a form of wrestling where the rules were that there were no rules. Well, actually, there were two: no gouging and no biting. Apart from that, it was anything goes! Not surprisingly, many competitors were known to have died. Unfortunately for the girls, married women weren't allowed to watch – although unmarried ones weren't barred. Unfortunately for the boys, competitors weren't allowed to wear clothes, so they all had to compete naked! In the end, Christianity put paid to the Olympics after 1,000 years in AD 393, because they were a Pagan event.

Nobody ever talks about the Dinolympics though, and they went on for millions of years! My favourite event was the velociraptoss. Seeing those little dinosaurs flying through the air is way more exciting than the javelin throw, believe me.

Next time you're bored at the theatre, blame the Greeks. They invented plays, and would have huge competitions to see who wrote the best ones. Only men could be actors, so they had to play the parts of all of the women too.

The Smashing Spartans

Ancient Greece was made up of a number of city-states, and for a long time Athens were the top dogs. Athenians were clever, sophisticated, witty... pretty boring in fact. Then came the Spartans, and they were horrible!

There was nothing the Spartans liked more than a good fight, and they fought a famous one at Thermopylae in 480 BC when the nasty Persians were invading with more than 100,000 men. Around 300 Spartans stood in their way and... well... they all died. But they held off the Persians for three days, which was pretty impressive, and their leader, Leonidas, was honoured as a hero.

If you think you've got it tough now, be glad you weren't a Spartan! When a child was born, if it looked a bit sick it would be taken away and left outside to die. Assuming you survived that foul treatment, at the age of seven children had to leave home and fend for themselves.

School included learning how to sleep outside, learning how to steal food and being the toughest, fastest, best fighter around.

It wasn't any easier for the girls. They had to learn to run, wrestle, throw javelins... and be a good housewife. And, so they didn't become vain, they weren't allowed any nice clothes. In fact, they weren't allowed any clothes at all! Until they were about 12 all Spartan children would be naked.

Dr Dino's Disgusting Story

The Spartans were a strange bunch. They were only interested in being warriors, and their code was written by an odd chap called Lycurgus. He decided that children shouldn't be given enough food, meaning they had to steal to survive. However, if they were caught they should be soundly beaten for stealing. The Spartans thought this was a smashing idea. He tells this story about the best way for a child to act:

'One day a child was so hungry he snuck into the nearest village and stole a fox. Alas, someone spotted him and thought he looked like he was up to something so they asked him what he was doing. The quick-thinking young man quickly hid the fox up his tunic and denied he had been doing anything wrong. They wouldn't let him go, though, and questioned him intensely until suddenly he fell down, dead. The fox had been scratching and biting at his stomach, but the boy was so tough that he didn't let on. This sort of bravery is exactly what Sparta needs.'

Spartans were so obsessed with fighting that they had a law stating you had to be a soldier until you were 60. All the farming and trading was done by slaves.

Now, if you have a sneaky suspicion that the Spartan women thought all the men were being silly acting as tough as they were, then think again. When the men went to war, the women had a saying: 'Return with your shield, or on it' – meaning if you don't win, you had better come back dead. Tough love!

DID ROMANS REALLY WASH THEMSELVES IN WEE?

The Glorious Greeks II

When it came to war, the other Greeks had a few tricks of their own up their sleeves... You've almost certainly heard of the old sneaky wooden horse trick at Troy, when the attackers built a big wooden horse and hid inside it until they were inside the city. But have you heard of Archimedes' burning mirrors? While his city of Syracuse was under siege, Archimedes created a wall of mirrors, which he used to focus the sunlight and set fire to the attacking ships. On reflection, what a clever chap!

The Greeks had other weapons up their sleeve when it came to warfare. They invented gruesome weapons such as the crossbow and the catapult to give their enemies a real battering.

Alexander the Great was a pretty good leader by all accounts. He took over as king of Macedonia (part of Greece) from his father (who was unfortunately assassinated – one of the pitfalls of being an ancient leader) at the young age of 20. By the time he was 30 he had conquered all of Persia and was attacking India. He had created one of the biggest empires of the ancient world. And by the time he was 32… he was dead! A short but spectacular reign.

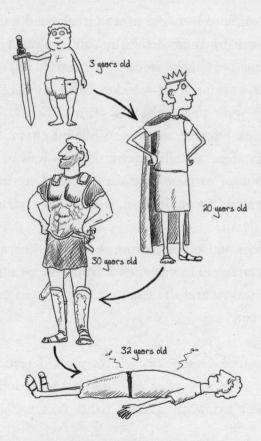

3 years old

20 years old

30 years old

32 years old

Dr Dino's Fun Fact

Alexander knew he was destined for greatness because he managed to untie the legendary Gordian knot, which meant he was to be the King of all Asia. He did cheat a little though… he simply sliced it in half with his sword!

The Greeks might have been pretty clever, but they still had some weird superstitions. They believed in augury, which basically meant checking out which way birds were flying and saying it was a sign. But, if they weren't satisfied with that, they would also kill the birds and pull out their guts. Then some clever chaps would examine them, believing they could tell the future from what they found!

The 10 Greatest Sayings No One Ever Said

10. 'Mirror, mirror, on the wall…' by The Queen in *Snow White and the Seven Dwarves*.
Everyone says this one wrongly. She actually said 'Magic mirror on the wall…' – the mirror knows it's a mirror, so why would she say it twice?

9. 'I only regret that I have but one life to give for my country' by Nathan Hale, an American revolutionary spy. Hale was captured by the British and hanged for his actions, and his famous 'last words' have been repeated by American soldiers for centuries. Unfortunately, there's no actual evidence he said them.

8. 'I disapprove of what you say, but I will defend to the death your right to say it' by Voltaire, the famous French philosopher.
History teachers love to give this quotation from Voltaire, but if yours ever does, ask them where he wrote it.

Because he didn't. Actually, it was a historian called Evelyn Beatrice Hall, writing about Voltaire, who used the line in 1906, more than 100 years later.

7. 'Because it's there' by George Mallory, mountaineer.
George Mallory, together with his companion Andrew Irvine, set out to be the first man to get to the top of Mount Everest. He might have made it, but we will never know – their bodies were found a few hundred metres from the summit decades later. When asked why he wanted to climb it, legend says he answered with the above. Actually, it was made up by an excitable newspaper reporter.

6. 'The end justifies the means' by Niccolo Machiavelli, a devious Italian.
Machiavelli wrote a book called *The Prince* in 1513 which was a guide for how to be a great ruler – in an evil genius kind of way. His basic idea was that it's much better to be feared than to be loved, but he never said 'the end justifies the means'. Although he probably thought it.

5. 'Elementary, my dear Watson' by Sherlock Holmes.
This is the most famous line said by Sherlock Holmes, and in pretty much every adaptation on TV or film you

will hear it at least once. However, this line never appears in the original stories written by Arthur Conan Doyle and was a much later invention.

4. 'Please, Sir, can I have some more?' by Oliver Twist in *Oliver Twist*.
Oliver Twist is given a bit too much credit for politeness in his most famous line, which people always get wrong. He actually said 'Please, Sir, I want some more.' _____

3. 'Houston, we have a problem' by Jim Lovell, astronaut on *Apollo 13*.
Do you want to be an astronaut? You can show off your space history the next time someone says this. Jim Lovell actually said 'Houston, we've had a problem.'

2. 'Lights, Camera, Action' by movie-makers everywhere.
Legend has it that directors always lead into a scene by saying 'Lights, Camera, Action.' However, this is never actually said on a real set.

1. 'Let them eat cake' by Marie Antoinette, the headless Queen of France.
History remembers her as being pretty insensitive to the starving masses, and your history teacher will probably

tell you that, when the queen was told that the peasants were starving because they didn't have enough bread, she replied 'let them eat cake.' However, this was actually said 100 years before by a different queen, and by all accounts Marie Antoinette was quite nice to the poor. Maybe not nice enough though, because during the French Revolution they were pretty quick to chop off the heads of both her and the king!

The Extraordinary Egyptians

The ancient Egyptians have the extraordinary honour of having the longest-lasting empire of all time. The Egyptian empire spanned more than 3,000 incredible years and began around 3,200 BC.

The pharaohs ruled Egypt, and they were a pretty powerful bunch. So powerful, in fact, that it was believed that they were gods, and their duties included praying every day to their fellow gods to make sure that the sun came up. (In fact, most pharaohs were a bit lazy and left it to their servants to do the praying. The sun still came up every day, so I guess the gods didn't mind too much.)

The pharaohs were always kings, but they weren't always men! Female pharaohs were quite rare, but they ruled as men, and they even wore fake beards to keep up the illusion for everyone. The most famous of these was Hatshepsut who was born around 1508 BC and is the

first woman ever recorded in history books. Her nephew Thutmose III tried to erase her name from everything after she died, but she was so successful as a ruler (much better than him anyway) that it survived.

Dr Dino's Pyramid Points

The pyramids are effectively massive tombs, as they were built to house the mummies of the dead pharaohs. There are more than 90 pyramids in Egypt and the biggest of them, the Great Pyramid, was built at least 4,500 years ago. They are so old that the ancient Greeks visited them as tourists!

The Egyptians believed that whatever you were buried with, you could take with you to the afterlife. So the pharaohs were buried with gold, jewels, food... and even a working toilet! It always pays to be prepared...

Unfortunately, building a great big pyramid and then burying a lot of treasure in it is like saying to a robber 'Look over here! Rob me!' They kept building bigger and more complicated pyramids to make it harder to break in, but the grave-robbers just kept getting smarter. Eventually the pharaohs simply gave up.

The pyramids are extraordinary. The Great Pyramid was built from 2.3 million stones, weighing about 2 tons. What's more, they were built so perfectly that they still survive basically intact today, 4,000 years later. The most extraordinary thing to consider though is how they managed to build the enormous structures when they hadn't even invented the wheel! Nobody knows how they managed to move the stones into place.

It might have been an honour to be a servant to a pharaoh, but it's an honour I could do without. Treasure wasn't the only thing the pharaohs were buried with... The first few pharaohs were pretty gruesome and they

buried their servants with them, just in case they were needed in the afterlife. Don't worry, they didn't bury them alive... they killed them all first! The later pharaohs were a lot nicer. They were buried with models of their servants and believed they would come alive (or become dead?) in the afterlife.

One of the biggest Egyptian myths is that the pyramids were built by slaves. In fact, the hard graft was done by peasant labourers who seem to have been pretty well looked after to keep them healthy for such an important job.

Over the years the pyramids have attracted some pretty weird legends. Even Napoleon visited them and claimed he had seen visions of the future when he was inside.

Maybe the most extraordinary suggestion was made by a scientist from Czechoslovakia called Karel Drbal who said that if you put a blunt razor inside a pyramid and left it there for a while it came out sharp. As a doctor, I can tell you that this is rubbish. The greatest myth, though, is the Curse of Tutankhamun...

In 1922 the tomb of Tutankhamun was uncovered – a great find because it was the first that hadn't been completely stripped bare by grave-robbers. Less than a year later Lord Carnarvon, the first man into the tomb, was bitten by a mosquito and died. Over the next few years many people associated with the archaeological mission died in mysterious circumstances and by 1930 the English press reported that there had been 21 victims of Tutankhamun's curse! A bit of digging (by a journalist, not the archaeologists) uncovered a few key facts that hadn't been checked properly. Namely that most of the victims had absolutely nothing to do with the tomb. One 'victim' just shared the same surname as the expedition leader, Carter. Despite this, many people still believe in the evil curse of the pharaohs.

Hieroglyphs, the Egyptian alphabet made up of funny pictures, probably weren't invented by the Egyptians. The chances are they were brought to Egypt by West

Asian invaders. In fact, historians believe that the first pharaohs might not have been Egyptians, but conquerors from Asia.

Egyptians were very fond of animals and kept many as pets. The most popular pets were cats, but dogs, hawks, baboons and lions were also kept. Unfortunately for the animals, they were often mummified along with their owner when they died.

The Egyptians liked to look good, and they were no strangers to make-up. Not only did the women use it, but the men wore make-up around their eyes and on their cheeks as well.

Queen Cleopatra was a famous Egyptian queen... but she wasn't actually Egyptian. She was Greek. We think of Cleopatra as young and beautiful, but writers at the time talked much more about how clever and wise she was. There was nothing clever about how she died, mind you! After Julius Caesar, her lover, was murdered she had to choose between Augustus and Mark Antony, the two pretenders for the top job of the Roman Empire.

She opted for Mark Antony, and she chose poorly, because Augustus defeated him and he had to flee. While on the run, Antony heard that Cleopatra had killed herself so he stabbed himself as well, but he was as bad at suicide as he was at war, because he only wounded himself. The still-alive Cleopatra heard what had happened and Mark Antony was brought to her, where he eventually did die. Then, finally, Cleopatra poisoned herself as well. She was the final pharaoh, and with her passing ended the long 3,000-year line.

How to make a mummy in five easy steps

1. Remove the internal organs. This is easily done by cutting the body open and taking out the liver, lungs, intestines and stomach (put them in a jar for safe-keeping). The brain is a bit tricky and you will need a big hook to reach in through the nose to then drag it out.

2. Stuff the skull with sawdust and then rub salt all over the body to help dry it out. Leave for 40 days.

3. Rub the body with oil and stuff it with straw and sawdust to keep it supple and life-like.

4. Use wax to seal up any incisions or wounds and place an amulet over them for good luck.

5. Finally wrap the body up with linen and put some more amulets in every so often for more good luck. Place a mask over the face and seal into the sarcophagus. There, easy-peasy. Now wash your hands.

NOTE: You need to build a pyramid first. This might take a bit longer.

Egypt is pretty hot and sandy and, while that's good for getting a tan, it is not very good for your eyes. Egyptian records reveal that eye disease was a very serious issue and there was a lot of attention given to finding cures. Would you like to try either of these?

1. What animal sees well in the dark? A bat. So what does it make sense to do if you're having trouble seeing? Just dab some bat's blood into your eyes and, hey presto, you should be cured!

2. If for some batty reason that doesn't work, find a pig and take its eyes out. Crush them up and mix with honey and lead. Take the mixture and inject it into your ears. You should be immediately cured.

The Sly Saxons

The Saxons were pretty sly. When you think of Vikings, what do you think of? Mean, smelly, vicious, stupid thugs who came and invaded England, pillaging and burning anything they could get their hands on, right? And what about the Saxons, the people who were led by Alfred the Great (for a while at least) and who the English are still named after (Anglo-Saxons)? Pretty decent chaps overall? Actually, you couldn't be more wrong!

When the Romans left England they left the Britons in charge. The Britons were having problems keeping out the troublesome Celts and Picts, so they invited two Saxon brothers over, Hengest and Horsa, to do the job for them. Unfortunately, Hengest and Horsa took one look around and quite liked what they saw. They invited their mates over and kicked out the Celts, the Picts... and the Britons! And they weren't very nice about it. In fact, they burned and pillaged their way through the country, causing a historian named Gildas to call them the worst thing that had ever happened to the country. Not so nice after all!

So why do we think of the Saxons as such good guys? Well, they were sly enough to realise that history will remember you better… if you write the history yourself! They wrote the Anglo-Saxon Chronicle, which tells the story of how great the sly Saxons were. Some of my fellow doctors and historians question how truthful they were, not least because many of the stories involve dragons.

Dr Dino's Most Important Saxon You Definitely Won't Ever Have Heard Of

Bede was a very clever but very dull Saxon monk. He spent all his time praying and writing, and historians love him because he wrote the first history of the English people. In fact, your history teacher will probably tell you he is the 'Father of English History'. BORING!

But he did something that changed the way the whole world worked, and that you use every single day. In his book he used the dating system AD and BC, which we all know today. Without him, 2014 would actually be 'the 62nd year of Queen Elizabeth's reign'. Imagine having to write that at the top of every piece of work!

You will probably have heard of Alfred the Great. A pretty good king, right? The Vikings had invaded and were bashing the Saxons left, right and centre. If it wasn't for the great warrior Alfred, England would probably be called Vikengland! Except that wasn't quite what happened...

Alfred got beaten by the Vikings and went on the run before he slyly gave them all his money to leave him alone for a while! Only after he had regrouped did he knock them over the head, win back the land he lost and create peace.

So why do we remember him as being so great? Well, he was pretty clever and decided that the best way to teach people what he had done would be to write his history himself. And he wasn't about to call himself Alfred the Average!

Saxon monks and nuns had a tough life. They had to say mass seven times a day, including in the middle of the night! They had to spend the rest of the time tending the flocks, looking after sick people or writing books and they even weren't allowed to speak during dinner! But some of them were a bit naughty... There were often complaints about monks who drank bottles and bottles of wine, had wives and kids, and even played sports and went fox-hunting. Maybe Bede wasn't so boring after all!

Monks wrote a lot, but they didn't have pens and paper. Instead they had to create their own and that was a lot more disgusting than chopping down trees, believe me! If you want to try to make some Saxon paper, here's what you have to do in five easy steps:

1) Take a lamb.
2) Kill the lamb. Preferably by cutting its throat.
3) Take the skin and clean it – both the nice, fluffy woollen side and the revolting bloody fleshy side.
4) Stretch it out so it's nice and tight.
5) Smooth the roughness out with a stone.

And voila! You should be left with the finest paper in the land.

Athelstan was Alfred the Great's grandson and when he became king England was still divided. In fact, there was no such thing as England yet. Athelstan was truly a great warrior though, and he defeated the Vikings in the Battle of Brunanburh – one of the most important battles in all of English history! It was after this that he became the very first King of England.

Athelstan's big problem was that he was too busy fighting and didn't do enough writing, so now nobody has ever heard of him! In fact, historians don't even know where Brunanburh is – most of them can't even pronounce it!

Saxons might have been sly, but they weren't very good doctors. Some of their favourite cures included yawning at holly to help toothache, eating the liver of a buck for night-vision loss and stopping bleeding with clots of horse poo. Spit, snails, wee and worms were all common ingredients used in many medicines.

The last Saxon king, Harold, famously died with an arrow through his eye at the Battle of Hastings in 1066. He might have had the last laugh over William the Conqueror in the end, though. William died of illness 21 years later, and the disease made his body swell up horribly. In fact, he grew so big that he wouldn't fit in his coffin and when they tried to force him into it his body exploded open, spreading a foul odour around the church. He probably had the fastest funeral of any English king!

Dr Dino's 10 Greatest Inventors of All Time

10. Benjamin Franklin was a busy man. Not only was he an inventor, author and politician, he was also one of the Founding Fathers of the USA. Among many other things, he invented the bifocals, helping millions to see. All that doesn't mean he didn't do stupid things though… Before inventing the lightning rod he tried an experiment to prove lightning was electricity – by flying a kite in the middle of a thunderstorm! He had a pretty hair-raising experience, but survived to invent another day.

9. Eureka! Around 250 BC Archimedes figured out how to measure the volume of things with water while lying in the bath and was so excited he ran down the street naked! He also invented Archimedes' Screw, which was one of the first contraptions to successfully move water upwards. And when he was in the besieged city of Syracuse he invented a huge claw that could lift ships out of the sea, and even a heat ray that could use sunlight to cause fires! All in all, a pretty cool guy.

8. John Logie Baird changed the world in 1925 when he broadcast the first live televised images. Without him there would be no TV, and life would be much more boring.

7. The Wright Brothers were pioneers of aviation and built the first powered airplane. Their first successful flight was in 1903 and the plane clocked in at a rapid speed of 6.8 miles per hour. You could almost walk quicker than that!

6. Hero of Alexandria was born in AD 10, about 1,750 years before the Industrial Revolution, but that didn't stop him from inventing a basic steam engine way before most people even knew what steam was. And he did much more than all that, inventing a windmill, a pump and even, most importantly, a vending machine.

5. Alexander Graham Bell invented the telephone, in one swoop changing the way the world communicated and putting the telegram out of business. And luckily for him he never had to worry about nagging calls from his mum or his wife because they were both deaf!

4. One of the most electrifying personalities of the 19th century was Thomas Edison who held an incredible 1,093 patents (these are the licences you get when you invent something). He invented the light bulb, the movie camera and the record player – pretty impressive, but not as impressive as...

3. Nikola Tesla. Tesla actually worked for Edison for years and spent most of his time making Edison's inventions better. He still had time to redesign the way electricity worked, create remote controls, neon lamps, X-rays and he also figured out radar 18 years before it was invented. The problem was that Edison was so jealous of him he spent all his time telling people to ignore Tesla and, because Edison was a bit of a bully, they believed him. And Tesla had the unfortunate habit of forgetting to write down how he invented something.

2. Leonardo da Vinci wasn't just an inventor. He was a painter, mathematician, musician, architect, botanist... you name it, he did it – the *Mona Lisa* was just one of his works of art. Although most of his inventions were never actually made, he came up with workable ideas for parachutes, helicopters, cannons, deep-sea diving suits and even tanks.

1. The greatest inventor of all time didn't even build anything. In 1989 a computer scientist called Tim Berners-Lee created the first webpage and invented the Internet. It has changed the world forever, and is used every day by billions of people around the world. In short, it's the best thing since sliced bread. And I love sliced bread.

Dr Dino's Favourite Invention

The fire hydrant has saved countless lives since it was invented, but nobody knows who to thank. The patent that showed who invented it was destroyed... in a fire!

The Virtuous
Victorians

Queen Victoria ruled for a long time – 64 years in fact, making her the longest-serving English monarch. She ruled so virtuously that the country grew rich and happy. Or at least some people did... the poor were still pretty unhappy. In fact, in 1842 a report showed that half of all children died before they reached five years of age!

Rich Victorians had more time for hobbies than anyone had before. Sports like cricket, rugby and football became much more serious and national leagues were formed. Novels were published by the thousands for people to read in their spare time. Gardening became something you did for fun, not just to grow crops. But there were some more unusual hobbies too:

1. Séances: the Victorians were very superstitious and loved trying to talk to the dead. Being a medium – someone who could 'communicate' with the dead – was a very lucrative business. Even the Queen was rumoured

to conduct séances to try to speak with her beloved Prince Albert.

2. Ratting: hygiene wasn't a strong point of the Victorians and there were plenty of rats running around the streets and sewers. Which was lucky, because they were needed for the sport of 'ratting'. To play, all you need is two dogs, a pit, fifty or so rats and a stopwatch. You throw the rats into the pit and then release the dogs – the winner is the dog who can kill the most rats in the time given! Does that sound like a fun way to spend a Saturday afternoon?

3. Fern hunting: international travel became possible for the average rich Victorian, and they were obsessed with bringing strange flowers and animals back from the exotic countries that they visited. The most bizarre of these collections were ferns… people would spend thousands of pounds to get the most exotic fern and then

they would spend the whole time showing it off to their friends. They should have seen some of the giant ferns us dinosaurs used to munch on...

4. Anthropomorphic taxidermy: a fancy way of saying collecting stuffed animals. But these were real animals and the Victorians loved dressing them up. They would even create little scenes such as guinea pigs playing cricket or cats in wedding dresses marrying each other... It's not quite Barbie and Ken!

5. Mourning: the Victorians were pretty death-obsessed and took mourning very seriously. Even Queen Victoria herself was a serious mourner – after Prince Albert died she went into seclusion and hardly made a public appearance for years. When she did she refused to wear a crown, preferring instead to put on a black mourner's headdress. The mourning process started well before burial and included some pretty weird stuff – not least the *memento mori,* which were bizarre family portraits taken AFTER someone in the family died, with the dead person having the central position! Dead central, obviously!

Dr Dino's Favourite Victorian Funeral Superstitions

When someone dies you have to stop the clocks in the room at the exact time of death, otherwise everyone will have bad luck.

Never wear new clothes to a funeral, especially shoes.

When a person dies all of the mirrors in the house have to be covered otherwise the dead person's soul could be trapped inside.

Victorians were so scared of being buried alive that they were watched for four days before burial just in case they were in a coma and they moved. Then a bell was installed in the coffin, so that if they woke up they could ring the bell and let people know they were buried alive!

When Victorians were in mourning they only wore black mourning dress and couldn't wear jewellery except for jewellery made with the hair of the person that died.

If a number of people die in the same family then you must tie a black ribbon to everything that goes in or out of their house, even animals. Otherwise the deaths will keep on spreading.

And finally... whenever you yawn you have to cover your mouth with your hand to stop your soul escaping. That might be easy enough for you – but I have pretty short arms!

One of the great inventions of all-time became common in the Victorian era – the flushing toilet. Before that people used to go in a bucket and then chuck it all out of the window. Eurgh!

Queen Victoria was a remarkable woman and one of the most successful monarchs of all time. Many of her subjects looked up to her... except when they met her. She was under five feet tall and, when she died, she had at least a 50-inch waist. That means she was as wide as she was tall!

The Victorians almost always wore black, but this wasn't just because they were in mourning. The Industrial Revolution was in full swing and the air was more polluted than your toilet seat. This meant that if you wore light clothes, by the end of the day they would look black!

Victorian women used to faint or 'swoon' a lot and, although you might think it was an act, they had a very good reason. Corsets were very fashionable in the 19th century, and they squeezed a woman's waist until it was half the size it was meant to be. In fact, it was so tight it actually rearranged their internal organs! Not surprisingly, this led to difficulty breathing and meant that women fainted any time they got out of breath!

The Victorian era was a time of great advances in science and medicine – they discovered what germs were, how vaccinations worked, how to use X-rays... but they still got a few things wrong:

1. They laced children's cough syrup with morphine – a powerfully addictive drug that makes you sleepy and sometime hallucinate. It stopped them coughing so much though!

2. If you thought the children's version was bad, adult coughs were treated with heroin.

3. Lobotomies were the answer to mental-health problems ranging from schizophrenia to depression. They worked. The problem was that these procedures worked by removing large chunks of your brain, making you incredibly stupid in the process!

4. If you were in pain and had a fever would you a) like to be in a warm bed, or b) like buckets of cold water thrown on you? If you answered 'b' then you are a true Victorian! Hydrotherapy was an extremely popular – but extremely ineffective – treatment for any number of illnesses.

If you don't feel like going into school tomorrow you should know who to blame... the Victorians! They were so virtuous that they introduced laws which meant that every child had to go to school and set up the first state schools so that even the poorest children didn't have an excuse.

Reckless Revolutions

Throughout the history of time civilisations have had one thing in common. At the top are the chosen few who pretty much have everything anyone could ever want and at the bottom are the millions of poor people who pretty much have... nothing. No wonder there have been so many revolutions when the rich people get too cocky for their own good! Maybe you could learn a thing or two for the next time your teacher looks a bit too cheerful when setting you homework...

Spartacus has to be known as the grandfather of revolutions. He was a gladiator in Rome and started a rebellion with other gladiators in protest at their treatment (their treatment being having to fight to the death – usually theirs!). Thousands of slaves joined him and for a couple of years he had an army so big that it seemed like the whole might of Rome couldn't defeat it. Unfortunately for Spartacus, it could... and in 71 BC

Spartacus was defeated. Legend has it he was so loved by his people that when the Romans asked 'Who is Spartacus?' his entire army answered 'I'm Spartacus!' so that they could never find and punish him. In reality, he probably died in battle and it wouldn't have mattered anyway because everyone was punished... all 6,000 survivors were crucified! Remind me never to get on the bad side of a Roman.

The Romans obviously weren't very popular because Boadicea led another major rebellion against them. She was the Queen of the Iceni (who lived in Norfolk), and she wasn't too keen on the Romans ruling Britain. Boadicea rebelled and was very successful – she even captured and destroyed London. Like Spartacus, eventually she was defeated. Nobody knows what happened to her, but she probably poisoned herself after the defeat. If you learn anything from her and Spartacus, it should be: don't rebel against the Romans!

The real Count Dracula was actually Vlad III, or Vlad the Impaler as he was known. He held the throne in Wallachia (Romania) three times because he kept getting kicked off and then having to lead a revolution to regain his power.

If you think the legendary Count Dracula is bad, he's

nothing compared to Vlad the Impaler. He earned his nickname because anyone who offended him he would impale with a stick through their stomach and leave them there for days. When one unfortunate chap complained about the smell from all the rotting bodies, Vlad thought he would help out – by impaling

I'm so thoughtful ...

him from the ceiling so he would be further away from them! It's thought he killed about 80,000 people during his various reigns.

The Peasant's Revolt of 1381 started because of heavy taxation, but was also probably an attack on the brutal system of serfdom (basically a fancy word for slavery) that the lords of England employed. The leader was a fellow called Wat Tyler, who was clever enough to lead his fellow rebels to London and storm the Tower of London. Unfortunately, he wasn't clever enough to see that agreeing to a meeting with the King on his own was a bad idea. You see, King Richard II was a master negotiator – his best trick was to chop the head off the other person! What an end for poor old Wat.

Dr Dino's Top Tip For a Revolution

When revolutions go right they can be glorious – especially for the people in charge, because they are the new top dogs! Like Napoleon or George Washington. However, get things wrong and you might not be too popular... just ask Guy Fawkes! His plan to blow up Parliament was discovered and he was executed for treason as a terrorist. Worse, he is burned every year on Bonfire night to remind everyone what a nasty guy he is.

So remember: the main difference between a heroic freedom fighter and a despicable terrorist is that one wins and the other doesn't – if you're going to revolt, make sure you're going to win first!

Martin Luther was a 16th-century priest who proved that revolutions don't have to be bloody – at least not at first. He hated the way Catholics used religion to make money and get power, so he nailed a list onto a church door saying how he wanted to change things – starting a protest movement that led to the 'Protest-ant' religion. This new religion transformed European politics and since then the battle between Protestants and Catholics has been very bloody indeed.

Oliver Cromwell successfully knocked Charles I off the throne – and his head off his shoulders. In the only period of English history when England didn't have a monarch, Cromwell served as Lord Protector of the Realm. He died and was buried, but Charles II was so angry he still wanted revenge... he had Cromwell's body dug up and beheaded! A warning – even if you lead a successful revolution you can still find yourself on a chopping block.

The American Revolution at the end of the 18th century ended up with the USA becoming independent and drawing up the US Constitution which declared all men free. Hooray! So long as you were white and male, that is... otherwise you weren't quite so free. Apparently 'equal rights' really meant 'equal rights for me, my friends and people like me. It would be really helpful if everyone else could cook and clean for us and not make too much of a fuss. Okay?'

The French Revolution was another glorious revolution. It started in 1789 and ended with everyone being 'equal'. But in this case, it was more like 'equally likely to have your head chopped off by the guillotine'. The revolutionaries started life with the pleasant execution of King Louis and his wife Marie Antoinette and everyone was pretty happy (well, not Louis and Marie Antoinette so much...), but then came The Terror. Tens of thousands of people were guillotined in Paris – everyone from the common people, to the aristocracy, and even the leader of the revolution

No pushing, you'll all get a turn.

himself, Robespierre. All of which goes to show, generally speaking, you should try not to be around for any period of time called 'Terror'.

Dr Dino's Did You Know?

Which revolution caused more deaths than the First World War and was possibly the second most deadly war of all time? Do you know? It was... the Taiping Rebellion! This little-known (at least, little-known outside of China) Chinese rebellion, which occurred in the 1850s, killed at least 20,000,000 people and some historians think it could have killed as many as 100,000,000. But I bet nobody in your class has even heard of it... As a test, next time your history teacher asks you a difficult question ask him what the most deadly rebellion was. If they don't get it right then it might be time for a little classroom revolution!

The Russian Revolution was led by a couple of men called Lenin and Trotsky and they helped overthrow the incredibly unpopular ruling Tsars. They founded the first Marxist state, and their motto was also equality for everyone, but these guys really meant it! Some people though were 'a bit more equal' than others. Meaning they weren't equal, they were in charge. In the end this revolution, which barely killed anyone at the time, killed tens of millions of people over the next 75 years, including Trotsky himself.

Ridiculous Romans

The Romans had a pretty big empire – in fact it stretched just about all the way around the known world at that point. But that didn't stop them getting up to some ridiculous behaviour. Even the way the city of Rome was founded is ridiculous...

They believed that twins, Romulus and Remus, were abandoned at birth and found by a pack of wolves that didn't gobble them up, but raised them as their own! When they were older the twins decided to build a new city but they couldn't decide where. They argued so much that Romulus ended up killing Remus before founding Rome... That's brotherly love!

You probably know all about gladiators fighting to the death in Rome (I imagine it's a bit like the school play-ground). But I bet you didn't know that the Romans believed that gladiators' blood could cure many diseases if you drank it... bleurgh!

The Romans were so ridiculous they didn't know when to stop eating. It was fashionable for rich people to hold lavish feasts that would last all day long and the munching would never stop. When you were full, you would run – or wobble – off to a little side room called a *vomitorium* and, well, vomit. Then you'd come back and carry on eating as if nothing had happened! Try that next time you're over at a friend's house at tea and see what their parents think...

Romans were obsessed with wee. They used it for everything... washing clothes, washing their hair – even as toothpaste!! To make sure they had enough they left pots on street corners for people to wee in whenever the need arose. Imagine what Roman towns smelled like...

This sounds absolutely ridiculous but, as a scientist, I have to point out that they had a reason. Soap hadn't been invented yet and wee contains ammonia, which does clean things and even makes your teeth whiter. All the same, I think I'd rather go to the dentist.

Dr Dino's Least Favourite Roman Joke

Question: What did the Roman Emperors use to wash themselves with?

Answer: The Royal Wee!

Next time you're invited to a fancy-dress party, don't go in a white toga – use your mum's favourite purple bedsheets instead. Purple was a very exotic colour for the Romans and emperors and senators only wore purple togas. In fact, nobody else was allowed to wear purple... if they did they would be charged with treason!

Dr Dino's Craziest Emperor

Rome had some ridiculous rulers in its time, but none more ridiculous than Caligula. He got a bit too big for his boots and had everyone worship him as a living God. Unfortunately (for his subjects), he was frequently angry and would kill for fun – he was once bored at the circus and ordered an entire section of the crowd to be thrown into the ring with lions for his entertainment.

Worse, he thought he was a comedian. Once, at a religious ceremony, a priest was waiting for him to hit an animal over the head with a hammer to sacrifice it, but Caligula thought it would be hilarious to knock the priest round the noggin instead. Ouch!

Probably the craziest thing he ever did though was try to have his horse appointed consul – the equivalent of Prime Minister. The Romans must have become bored of having such a ridiculous leader, though, because in AD 41 he became the first Roman Emperor to be assassinated. Good riddance!

The Romans were incredible builders and they devised clever systems to heat under their floors (hint: it helped that they had a lot of slaves to keep a fire going... so not *that* clever). It's well known that they spent a lot of time at their baths, but what's less well known is that they were the first civilisation to use indoor public toilets – and they loved hanging out there! Maybe they were just waiting to use someone's wee for a bit of mouthwash...

You might think you know a lot about Julius Caesar. After all, he's pretty famous – he even has the month of July named after him (I'm waiting for the month of Dinember to be recognised... any Dinhour now I think). But did you know that Caesar probably never said 'Et tu, Brute?' after he was stabbed? Or that Caesar was captured by pirates for ransom and, when they named a price for him, he was insulted by how low it was and demanded they ask for more? He had the last laugh... after he was freed he hunted down the pirates and had them all executed.

Things were pretty tough in Roman schools – you would only get one day off a week and, if your teacher thought you were being lazy, they were allowed to whip you! The good news was only the rich kids had to go to school. The bad news was if you weren't at school that meant you had to work! And the Romans had some ridiculous jobs. There was one person whose only job was to pluck people's armpit hairs! School doesn't seem so bad now, does it?

The Frighteningly Great First World War

The First World War is also known as the Great War (it wasn't as great as the Great Sauropod Wars, but I won't go into that). Whoever named it probably wasn't a soldier though... it wasn't so great for the unfortunate people who had to fight in it! The enemy were the least of their problems. The soldiers also had to worry about wet trenches, trench foot, lice, Spanish flu, incompetent generals and shellshock. A pretty easy life then!

Private George Ellison joined the army in 1914 and fought in many of the major battles for four years until the very last day of the war when, unfortunately, he was killed. He was the last British casualty, but he wasn't the only person to die that day – in all, 11,000 men died on the same day as George. The frightening thing was that they didn't need to... the armistice (which agreed the end of the war) was signed at five in the morning, but someone thought it would be great to end it on the

11th hour of the 11th day of the 11th month of the year. Those 11,000 people never had to die.

The greatest explosion of the war was set off by the British when they packed more than 1,000,000lbs of explosives under Messines Ridge, in Belgium. At least 6,000 Germans died in the blast and the explosion was so loud it could be heard all the way across the channel in London.

Some of the explosives used in the attack never exploded, and are still there – with some of them buried underneath a farm! In 1955 a lightning bolt struck the ground and caused a 'small' amount (40,000lbs!) to explode. Luckily, the only casualties were cows, and the farmer dined out on steak that night.

The First World War saw many new weapons invented, such as the flamethrower, the submarine and the tank. These were incredibly frightening on the battlefield although the people who made the first British tank didn't think too much of it... they called it 'Little Willie'. The name tank was invented because the British tried to disguise them as water storage tanks so the enemy wouldn't see them coming!

The royal family weren't always called Windsor. At the start of the First World War, the royal family name was Saxe-Coburg-Gotha, which is a Germanic name. So Germanic, in fact, that the royals thought they had better change it in case people started thinking they were the enemy.

The trenches were bad places to live... they were wet and muddy and filled with lice and rats. What's worse, the bunkers where the soldiers slept were poorly built and would often be destroyed during enemy artillery fire. Or at least, the British trenches were bad... The German trenches were far better and had bunk beds, cupboards, water taps, electric lights and even doorbells! Much more civilised.

The average life expectancy in a trench was just six weeks, which, you'll agree, isn't what you want to hear when you sign up for the army. But if you thought you might fancy a transfer to the RAF, think again. The average life expectancy for a pilot was around two weeks.

In all, just fewer than 10,000,000 men died in the fighting. While this was bad, it was nothing compared to the Spanish Flu which around the same time killed 50–100,000,000 people. Imagine how annoyed you would be if you fought for four years, finally made it home, caught the flu and croaked!

The First World War saw the first bombing raids by airplanes. Parisians were pretty worried about this because their city was right in the firing line, so they came up with a pretty great idea: build a fake Paris! They built a dummy city just to the north of the real one in the hope the bombers would get confused and attack the wrong one. Regrettably, it took so long to make that it wasn't finished by the end of the war and so we'll never know how tricky it really was.

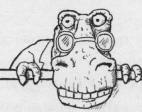

Dr Dino's Day of Humanity

As a dinosaur, it's easy to judge humans too harshly. After all, we didn't always get on terribly well with each other. But all the same, wars like this one are terrible affairs, which is why Christmas Day 1914 is so important...

A Christmas Day truce was announced, and soldiers on the front line put down their guns to sing carols to each other, swap gifts such as tobacco, food and drink, play football and even cut each other's hair! For one day, everybody was friends, and many of the soldiers wrote home to say how wonderful it was. The very next day, though, it was back to business as usual. What's worse, the Generals didn't approve of the festive ceasefire... in 1915 they ordered anybody who tried to call a truce to be shot on the spot.

While the British royal family sat comfy at home in their palace (having made the sacrifice of changing their name) the Belgian royal family made a real sacrifice. King Albert led the army personally from the trenches and his 14-year-old son became a Private in the army too. Even his wife, the queen, worked as a nurse helping the soldiers. At the end of the war he returned to Brussels victorious to a true hero's welcome, and he deserved it!

Fighting in the air might have been dangerous, but at the start of the war it was fairly basic. In those days, the planes didn't have weapons attached to them and the pilots would shoot guns like pistols at each other out of the cockpits.

As if being shot at and shelled wasn't bad enough, the soldiers of the First World War had something else to contend with – gas attacks. And this wasn't like being in the same room as your brother after a particularly large portion of beans... although that can be bad enough! In all, 100,000 people died as a result of gas attacks, and many more were wounded. There was one huge problem though. The success of such an attack depended on the wind blowing the gas the right way towards the enemy. On occasion, the wind would change and the gas would come floating back, gassing your own soldiers!

Probably the only thing worse than being gassed was the way to stop it: before gas masks were handed out, soldiers were told to protect themselves by covering their mouths with a cloth... soaked in wee! Eww!

Pilots in the First World War had a lot of problems, but none were more urgent than the one caused by inhaling castor oil. It was used as an engine lubricant, but the fumes have an unfortunate side-effect – they cause constant diarrhoea! I wouldn't have liked to be in one of their cockpits on a long flight...

The Spectacular Seas

Since humans can't swim nearly as well as we dinosaurs can, you've always had a funny relationship with the seas. Whereas we would just go swimming happily around wherever we wanted, you can't get anywhere without boats. This has meant that traditionally the seas have been a place of wonder, of danger, of adventure and most of all, of seasickness.

The seas can be dangerous, but there are some spectacular young sailors who have managed to go right around the world all on their own. Two 16-year-old girls have made the trip: Laura Dekker was the youngest, but took 366 days to do it, while Jessica Watson took only 209 days to complete her journey. As a responsible doctor, I would suggest not attempting to go right around the world on your first attempt though.

The US Navy lost one of its biggest ships, the USS

Cyclops, in 1918 with all of the 306 crew on board simply disappearing without a trace. Nobody quite knows what happened because, even though it was during the First World War, no German ships could be linked with sinking it. However, investigation later showed that the captain was an unstable man who had actually been born in Germany and had strong connections to Germany, so there's a good chance he might have sunk the ship on purpose!

Many people get a bit seasick, but the sailors of the British Navy might have had another reason for feeling a bit queasy. Until 1970, they received a daily ration of one-eighth of a pint of rum. It was a sad day for the tipsy sailors when the practice was abolished.

Dr Dino's Top Three Shipwrecks

3. *Mary Rose* – She was one of the finest ships of the 16th century, and led a distinguished military career as the jewel in the crown of the British Navy. However, she came to quite an undistinguished end. While advancing into battle against the French, she turned too sharply and simply toppled over under the weight of all of her cannons! Most of the 400-plus crew couldn't swim and all but 35 perished. The *Mary Rose* has since been recovered and more than 19,000 well-preserved Tudor artefacts were found... so not all bad then!

2. In 1945, as the Second World War was coming to a close, the Germans evacuated Poland. One ship, the MV *Wilhelm Gustloff*, was crammed full of people; the majority were civilians but there were quite a few army and navy personnel on board too. Regrettably, they came across a Soviet submarine which torpedoed the ship, sinking it very quickly. Of the 10,600 people on board, 9,400 died, making it by far the worst disaster on the high seas ever.

1. The *Titanic* – Everybody knows the story of the *Titanic*, the so-called unsinkable ship that proved all too sinkable! All told, 1,517 people died when she struck an iceberg in the middle of the Atlantic Ocean. But I bet you didn't

know these facts from Dr Dino's learnatorium: there may not have been enough room on the lifeboats for everyone, but three dogs still found their way onto the boats and survived; we think of the *Titanic* as being spectacular, but actually it was cramped and horrible for most of the people on it, as the 700 third-class passengers only had two baths between them; at the time the *Titanic* wasn't that big a deal, the real celebrity boat was its sister boat, the *Olympic*.

The Vikings loved their longships, and warriors would pretty much live on them in order to go raiding (as the Saxons found out pretty quickly!). They weren't too worried about comforts and the ships were quite uncomfortable places without any... facilities. Whenever the Vikings wanted to go to the toilet, they just had to go over the side!

One of the most unusual sea battles was fought between a Brazilian and Uruguayan ship in the 1860s. The Uruguayans had run out of cannonballs and things were looking pretty hairy. Then, some bright spark realised they had a lot of stale cheese in their hold. They loaded up the cannon and fired the smelly ammunition at the Brazilians and somehow scored a couple of direct hits. The Brazilians

Run, they're armed with stale bread!

Painful Pirates...Aaaarr!

Picture a pirate. Do you see a big guy with a bushy beard, a peg-leg, a parrot on his shoulder and an eye-patch, who says 'aaaarr' before every sentence? If so, forget it... that's not how pirates used to look – that's just how Hollywood shows them. The first 'pirate' to say 'aaaarr' was actually Robert Newton, an actor who played Blackbeard in a movie in 1950.

Pirates may have seemed like a pretty lawless bunch, but actually they had very strict rules. Each ship would have its own Code of Conduct and everybody on board had to sign up to it. The Code would include rules such as no fighting with each other, no stealing from each other, and even no lying. Basically, everything they did to everyone else, they couldn't do to each other. Punishments for breaking these rules were very harsh.

The favourite punishment for a pirate was, as everyone

knows, to walk the plank. Except it wasn't... there are only a couple of mentions of this ever happening. More common was whipping, being marooned on a desert island or being keel-hauled – where the offender is thrown off the ship tied to a rope and then dragged under the ship. I'd prefer the plank!

The Jolly Roger flag, with its menacing skull and cross-bones, was used by pirates, but it wasn't the scariest version. That award goes to the blood-red 'No Quarter' flag. If a sailor saw one of those approaching they did their best to run pretty sharpish... it meant that the pirates would leave no survivors.

If you're hoping to make your fortune by seeking out some dead pirate's buried treasure then think again. There is very little evidence to suggest pirates buried treasure and even less that they made maps to tell everyone where they had buried it, which, when you think about it, is about the last thing you would do... Simply, the pirates were so intent on spending their new-found loot that there was never any left to bury!

It was bad luck for women to step foot on board a pirate ship, so normally it was a men-only profession. However, some of the most famous pirate captains ever were women, such as Ann Bonny and Mary Read, who were incredibly successful pirates and made a lot of the male captains pretty jealous.

Dr Dino's Dastardly Privateers

Do you know the difference between a pirate and the Royal Navy? The answer is… nothing! The British government would issue letters authorising certain ships to become privateers and attack 'enemy' (any foreigners they came across) ships whenever they wanted. They would take the loot just like regular pirates, except it would go in the Crown's pocket.

A famous example of this is Sir Francis Drake who, had he been a pirate, would have been known as one of the most evil, dastardly pirates there ever was. Because he was a privateer, though, he was seen as a hero in England. Over in Spain, whose ships he went after, they didn't quite see it the same way…

Pirates had a notoriously short life-span. Most were only active for a couple of years before they were either captured and executed, or retired to spend their earnings in peace. Blackbeard himself, the most famous pirate of them all, was only a pirate for around three years.

Many pirates pierced their ears and put precious studs or rings in them. This wasn't because they thought they looked nice though. For some reason, they believed that if they had silver or gold in their ears then they could see much better than without.

The Turbulent Tudor Family

The Tudors ruled England for quite some time, and they had some real characters in their family. They didn't always get on...

Henry VIII

Henry VIII is often thought of as one of the greatest rulers of England, although everyone knows about his marital troubles. He saw himself as a 'renaissance man', an educated, cultured ruler who was as interested in music and the arts as he was in hunting and war. In a lot of ways this was true: he was a great hunter, held lavish feasts, composed his own songs, paid for many artists to work... and so he's remembered fondly. But he had his flaws too...

1. Money – Henry VII was a very wise king and left his son with a wealthy, relatively peaceful kingdom. Henry VIII, however, loved the idea of war and spent years

fighting the French. He didn't really manage to win anything though, but he did pretty much bankrupt the country in the process.

2. Executions – It's hard to know exactly how many people Henry executed, but it certainly didn't stop with just his wives. In fact, Henry was a strong believer in getting his five a day... Not fruit and vegetables though, but executions! It's believed he had up to 72,000 people killed during his reign, which works out to about five a day.

I'm afraid that we can't do any more today, Sire. The axe has worn out.

3. Changing to Protestantism – Before I have angry Protestants attacking my learnatorium, it's important to say that Protestantism isn't a bad thing. But forcing a whole country to change their religion just because you don't fancy your wife anymore – and then chopping off your new wife's head anyway – isn't the best way to rule.

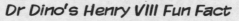

Dr Dino's Henry VIII Fun Fact

Henry was a notorious hypochondriac (meaning he always thought he was sick even when he wasn't. I know a few kids who become hypochondriacs right before school…). He didn't look after his health very well though… by the time of his death he weighed more than 300lbs! He was almost certainly the fattest king of England ever.

Bloody Mary

Mary I was Henry's oldest daughter and became queen after his son, Edward, died at the age of 16 (he was even less healthy than Henry!). The problem was that Mary was a Catholic, so England had to switch religions again... not so good for all the people who had declared they were now Protestants.

Queen Mary was the first woman to be crowned Queen of England.

Mary is known as Bloody Mary because when she became queen she started a vicious campaign against the Protestants, burning at the stake anyone who defied her as an example to others. But does she deserve her title?

I'm just misunderstood.

Well... your history teacher (and anyone she burned at the stake) will probably tell you yes, but really she didn't. She had 277 people executed in about four years, less than one every four days – hardly anything compared to her dear dad! So why is she called Bloody Mary? Because the Catholics lost in the end... and the Protestants didn't remember her as a very sympathetic person when they wrote history.

Dr Dino's Mary I Fun Fact

Despite being very religious, Mary loved to gamble. Unfortunately, she wasn't very good at it... records show one day she gambled away all the money she had on her and asked the servants for a loan so she could gamble some more. They refused... wisely. She bet the next day's breakfast instead and, as the accounts reveal, the next morning breakfast was on her!

Elizabeth I

Queen Elizabeth ruled for 45 years and, by all accounts, she was a pretty good queen. Of course, it helped that those accounts were written by Protestants who liked her, but still... pretty good. However, the fact that she was a Protestant meant that England had gone from Catholic to Protestant and back again all in about 30 years. That might not seem like such a big deal to you, but when you think you could lose your head if you forgot which one you were meant to be, it was a pretty turbulent time for the Tudor peasants!

Despite being such a good ruler, Elizabeth failed in what might be seen as her main duty – to have a child. She was nicknamed the Virgin Queen because in 70 years she was never married, although she was proposed to at least 25 times! The problem was that after she died there was no natural heir, meaning there was the potential for a civil war.

In paintings, Elizabeth is normally shown to be very, very pale. That wasn't because she never went to the beach but because she used to paint her face with white lead! This was a result of having smallpox when she was younger and being embarrassed about the scars left on her face.

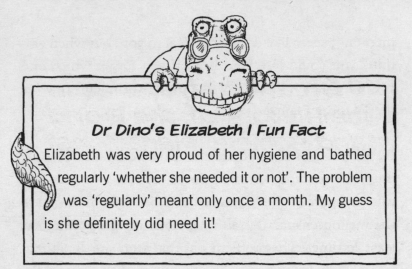

Dr Dino's Elizabeth I Fun Fact

Elizabeth was very proud of her hygiene and bathed regularly 'whether she needed it or not'. The problem was 'regularly' meant only once a month. My guess is she definitely did need it!

10 Greatest Mysteries in the History of the World (and some explanations)

Throughout history there have been many events that have left people scratching their heads and asking 'WHAT??!!' Fortunately, I am a scientist and a doctor, and I've devoted a considerable part of my learnatorium to figuring out exactly what's behind some of the greatest mysteries of all time.

10. Ball Lightning – This is one of the strangest natural phenomena that we know of. Everybody's seen lightning, but ball lightning is a much rarer, and cooler, variety. For centuries people have reported seeing strange orbs of light floating through the sky during thunderstorms. Unfortunately, they are deadly to touch and occasionally float their way into houses, killing everyone inside...

Up until now, we scientists had little idea why this happened, and only our friend Tesla, the inventor, could recreate it in a lab – but he never bothered writing down how! The answer is probably very boring and to do with silicon in soil... but floating lightning is an electrifying subject!

9. The Voynich Manuscript – This is a 240-page illustrated book that has recipes, astronomy, medicine, herbal remedies... all sorts. The problem is that nobody can read it! We know what it's about because of the pictures, but nobody knows who wrote it, where it's from, what the language is... anything! The best code-breakers in the world have tried to figure it out, even in my learnatorium, but they've not been able to read a single word.

8. Atlantis and Helike – Atlantis was an island mentioned by Plato that hosted a huge civilisation. It was destroyed by Athens in a war, sank beneath the sea and people have been searching for it ever since. They've never found it though, and with good reason... because Plato made it up! There was an ancient Greek city called Helike, though, which disappeared overnight in 373 BC and for a long time nobody knew why... until it was rediscovered in 2001. There was a huge earthquake and accompanying tsunami which buried the city at the bottom of a lake... The Real Atlantis! Not much comfort for all the people who lived there though...

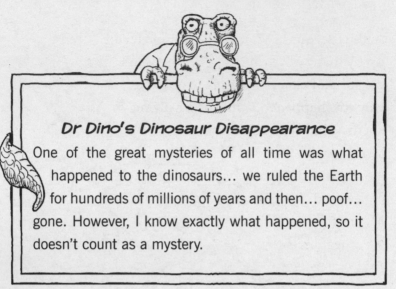

Dr Dino's Dinosaur Disappearance

One of the great mysteries of all time was what happened to the dinosaurs... we ruled the Earth for hundreds of millions of years and then... poof... gone. However, I know exactly what happened, so it doesn't count as a mystery.

7. Spontaneous Combustion – In the 19th century there were hundreds of reports of spontaneous human combustion, where people would catch fire and burn to death for no reason! Because most people who died were old and alcoholics, scientists thought that the alcohol in their bodies caught fire. What they didn't think of was that most of them smoked cigarettes or had candles next to them and being old and drunk makes it hard to run away from fire... Not so spontaneous after all!

6. The Bermuda Triangle – In 1950 a man called Edward Van Winkle Jones noticed many planes and ships were mysteriously disappearing in an area that became known

as the 'Bermuda Triangle', a claim backed up by many, many others over the years. All sorts of claims were made about why this happened... mostly involving aliens... but research at the learnatorium has led me to a different conclusion. It's not real! Most of the unexplained disappearances couldn't be explained because they never happened... conspiracy theorists just made them up. Mystery solved!

5. Stonehenge and the Carnac Stones – These ancient sites are a real mystery. Well Stonehenge isn't so much... it was built around 4,500 years ago, almost certainly for ancient religious reasons. What is truly befuddling is why the builders dragged the stones 100 miles across the country when there was plenty of stone nearby! The Carnac Stones in France are far more confusing... they are 3,000 prehistoric stones standing in France which are about 6,500 years old. Legend had it that the stones were a Roman legion that Merlin turned to stone.

Which is, of course, hogwash. Many explanations have been given for them, including them being a druid site, a representation of stars, or some sort of astronomical calendar. But the best is that they might have been an early earthquake warning system! We will probably never know...

4. Amelia Earhart – She was the most famous pilot in America in the 1930s and set off to become the first person to fly solo around the world. Sadly, she didn't make it. On the final leg of the trip, over the Pacific Ocean, she disappeared. Even though the search started just an hour later, no sign of her was ever found. There are all sorts of theories: that Amelia landed on a Japanese island and was an undercover American spy, that she landed there and was executed, that she crashed in Papua New Guinea or that she was bored of her fame and 'disappeared' to change her name. Seeing as her last message basically said 'I'm lost and low on fuel', the chances are that sadly she just ran out fuel and is now somewhere at the bottom of the Pacific Ocean.

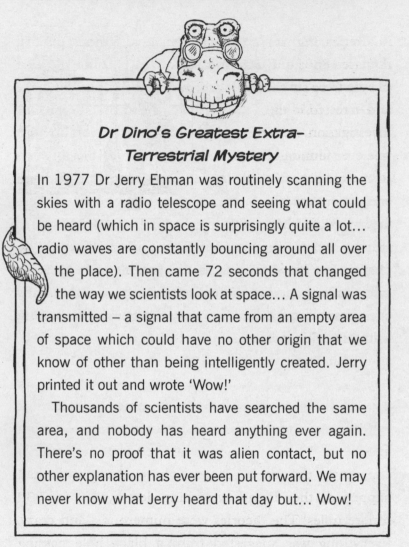

Dr Dino's Greatest Extra-Terrestrial Mystery

In 1977 Dr Jerry Ehman was routinely scanning the skies with a radio telescope and seeing what could be heard (which in space is surprisingly quite a lot... radio waves are constantly bouncing around all over the place). Then came 72 seconds that changed the way we scientists look at space... A signal was transmitted – a signal that came from an empty area of space which could have no other origin that we know of other than being intelligently created. Jerry printed it out and wrote 'Wow!'

Thousands of scientists have searched the same area, and nobody has heard anything ever again. There's no proof that it was alien contact, but no other explanation has ever been put forward. We may never know what Jerry heard that day but... Wow!

3. Jack the Ripper – London's most famous serial killer, Jack the Ripper may never be caught. He was involved

in a series of gruesome murders in the late 1880s but, although many people were suspected and arrested in the investigation, nobody was ever found guilty. Ripperologists, as they are known, are still fascinated and have

Lovely evening for a stroll, sir.

lengthy debates about whodunit but, incredibly, nobody even knows how many people he killed. It could be as many as around 15 or only a couple... because of a lack of forensic evidence it's impossible to be sure. One thing I am sure about though is he will never be unmasked, and the mystery will live on.

2. The Tunguska Event – On 30 June 1908 a huge explosion was reported in the air over a remote region in Siberia. When investigators arrived (10 years later... apparently nobody cared enough to check what had happened) they found everything destroyed... for 830 square miles! The theories were numerous – and crazy. Everything was suggested from a black hole passing through Earth to a huge bubble of natural gas exploding. Our old friend Nikola Tesla was even blamed by people

thinking he'd performed a secret experiment that went wrong. The most likely explanation is that a comet exploded when it hit the Earth's atmosphere.

To put into perspective how big this explosion was, it had the power of 1,000 Hiroshima bombs! Incredibly, nobody died in this explosion, because Siberia is so remote, but had it happened in London then the entire city would have been destroyed!

1. The *Mary Celeste* – This is probably the biggest mystery ever. On 5 December 1872, John Johnson spotted a ship floating on the high seas and decided to investigate. The ship was empty... of people at least. Everything was exactly as it should have been: the cargo was in place, the crew's valuable belongings were untouched, there was no sign of a struggle... but no sign of a crew either! They all disappeared and were never seen again.

Researchers have suggested piracy and mutiny, but there was no sign of a struggle. The cargo was alcohol, and nine barrels were empty, so some have suggested they got too drunk and fell overboard... but the captain never drank alcohol. The best and most interesting explanation, which has the Dr Dino Endorsement of Truth, is this: one lifeboat was missing. The alcohol leaked and the fumes spread through the ship. This is flammable, but burns at a very low temperature, so if it sparked it would create a huge explosion – but do no damage! The crew were superstitious and might have thought the ship was cursed, and so they fled in the lifeboat, which hit a storm and sank. It's because of peculiar things like this that we dinosaurs decided never to build boats...

No mystery is too great for Dr Dino's learnatorium! Now see if I've helped to demystify things for you by having a go at my quiz. Good luck...!

Quiz

1. What did the Aztecs use to make cakes?
   A. Mud; B. A sacrifice's heart; C. Pond-scum;
      D. Chocolate.

2. If you were a Spartan girl, what would you learn in
   school?
   A. How to fight; B. How to cook; C. How to sprint;
      D. All of the above.

3. In the First World War, what was the average life
   expectancy of a fighter pilot?
   A. Two hours; B. Two days; C. Two weeks; D. Two
   months.

4. Who was (probably) the first European to discover
   North America?
   A. Leif Ericson; B. Christopher Columbus;
      C. Francis Drake; D. George Washington.

5. Until gas masks were available, what was the best way to avoid poison gas attacks?
    A. Placing a cloth soaked in wee over your mouth; B. Holding your breath; C. Covering yourself in mud; D. There wasn't one.

6. What was the point of the Pyramids?
    A. For fitness training; B. As a tall lookout post; C. A big theatre was inside; D. As a tomb for the pharaoh.

7. What did Hero of Alexandria invent in the 1st century?
    A. Sandwiches; B. Vending machines; C. Helicopters; D. A primitive TV.

8. Who raised Romulus, the founder of Rome?
    A. His parents; B. His brother Remus; C. A pack of wolves; D. His best friend, Joe.

9. What happened to William the Conqueror at his funeral?
    A. He disappeared; B. He exploded; C. His head fell off; D. He woke up.

10. Why did the Victorians normally wear black?
    A. They thought it looked good; B. So the dirt
    wouldn't show; C. They had an obsession with
    vampires; D. It was cheaper.

11. What did Julius Caesar do with the pirates who
    captured him?
    A. Asked them to join his army; B. Forgave them;
    C. Made them apologise; D. Executed them.

12. Why did the Royal Family change their name to
    Windsor?
    A. It had a nice ring to it; B. They really liked
    Windsor Castle; C. They lost a bet and had to
    change it; D. Their previous name sounded too
    German.

13. What did contestants have to wear during the
    ancient Olympics?
    A. Full armour; B. A toga; C. Nothing; D. Women's
    clothing.

14. How did Vlad, the original Dracula, like to kill his
    victims?
    A. Chop them into little pieces and eat them;

B. Guillotine them; C. Drink their blood; D. Impale them.

15. What is mysterious about the Voynich Manuscript?
    A. It was written before books were invented;
    B. Nobody can read it; C. It's written in invisible ink; D. It predicts the future.

16. Where were the oldest human fossils found?
    A. The Pit of Bones; B. The Lair of Remains; C. The Hole of Humans; D. The Den of Skeletons.

17. What did Mary I lose in a bet?
    A. Her throne; B. Buckingham Palace; C. Breakfast; D. Her head.

18. If a Mayan's head was too broad what would they do to that person?
    A. Chop the head off; B. Squash the head between two pieces of wood; C. Worship them as a god; D. Exile them forever.

19. What did Saxon monks write on?
    A. Paper; B. Papyrus; C. The back of their hand; D. Lambskin.

20. What did the Uruguayans use to beat off the Brazilian navy in the 19th century?
A. Balls of cheese; B. Slingshots; C. Their ship as a battering ram; D. The ship's cat.

Answers

1.	C	11.	D
2.	D	12.	D
3.	C	13.	C
4.	A	14.	D
5.	A	15.	B
6.	D	16.	A
7.	B	17.	C
8.	C	18.	B
9.	B	19.	D
10.	B	20.	A